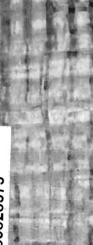

All royalties from this book will be donated to
THE ERIC CARLE MUSEUM OF PICTURE BOOK ART,
which was founded by Eric and Barbara Carle to inspire a
love of art and reading through picture books.

Visit the Eric Carle Museum of Picture Book Art
in Amherst, Massachusetts, or at carlemuseum.org.

Permission to reproduce the following is gratefully acknowledged:
"Caterpillars" © 2018 by Eric Carle; "Praying Mantis" © 2018 by Denise Fleming; "Moths" © 2018 by Teagan White;
"Dragonfly" © 2018 by Beth Krommes; "Katydid" © 2018 by Maggie Rudy; "Daddy Longlegs" © 2018 by Scott Magoon;
"Bees" © 2018 by Molly Idle; "Ants" © 2018 by Ekua Holmes; "Ladybug" © 2018 by Tim Hopgood; "Firefly" © 2018 by Kenard Pak;
"Peacock Spiders" © 2018 by Brendan Wenzel; "Millipedes" © 2018 by Britta Teckentrup; "Worker Bee" © 2018 by Eric Fan;
"Walking Stick" © 2018 by Eugene Yelchin; "Rhino Beetle" © 2018 by Joey Chou.

Henry Holt and Company, *Publishers since 1866*
Henry Holt® is a registered trademark of Macmillan Publishing Group, LLC
175 Fifth Avenue, New York, NY 10010 • mackids.com

ISBN 978-1-250-15175-9
Library of Congress Control Number 2017957952

Our books may be purchased in bulk for promotional, educational, or business use. Please contact your local bookseller
or the Macmillan Corporate and Premium Sales Department at (800) 221-7945 ext. 5442 or by e-mail at
MacmillanSpecialMarkets@macmillan.com.

First edition, 2018
Printed in China by RR Donnelley Asia Printing Solutions Ltd., Dongguan City, Guangdong Province

1 3 5 7 9 10 8 6 4 2

Eric Carle and Friends

What's Your Favorite Bug?

Joey Chou • Eric Fan • Denise Fleming • Ekua Holmes

Tim Hopgood • Molly Idle • Beth Krommes • Scott Magoon

Kenard Pak • Maggie Rudy • Britta Teckentrup

Brendan Wenzel • Teagan White • Eugene Yelchin

GODWINBOOKS

Henry Holt and Company

NEW YORK

CATERPILLARS
Eric Carle

To tell you the truth, I have not always cared for caterpillars. They are squishy and hairy and occasionally, when you hold them in your hand, they poop. Why, then, is the caterpillar my favorite bug? Many years ago, when I punched holes into a stack of paper, it made me think of a bookworm. But with the help of my good editor Ann Beneduce, *The Very Hungry Caterpillar* was born.

Now not only children love my book, but so do adults, who grew up with it a generation ago and still remember the caterpillar story with genuine affection. It has been translated into sixty-two languages—most recently Mongolian.

That's why I love caterpillars.

Praying Mantis

Denise Fleming

The praying mantis can easily hide in plants because its legs look like stems and its body looks like leaves. It is also the only insect that can turn its head and look right at you!

i like

MOTHS.

they come out
at night and
make the dark
less lonely.

Teagan White

DRAGONFLY

Beth Krommes

Dragonflies symbolize courage, strength, and happiness. Many are iridescent and colorful, shimmering like jewels in the sunshine. Fierce hunters and fast fliers, they can zoom in any direction, including backward and sideways. Best of all, dragonflies eat mosquitoes.

KATYDID

MAGGIE RUDY

Who hid in the trees, disguised as a leaf?

Katydid!

Who had ears on his elbows?

Katydid!

Who washed his face like a cat?

Katydid!

Who played his wings like a fiddle?

Katydid!

What song did he sing?

Katydid! Katydid! Katydid!

Hiding in my shady spot, playing hide-and-seek

(under our deck or at the wall),

I'd remain long after I heard someone speak—

late afternoon shadows began to fall.

"Come on; we're done playing!" the voice long begs.

No way, I thought to myself, you have to find me

Scott Magoon

DADDY
LONGLEGS

Bees

Molly Idle

Everybody knows that bees make honey. But did you know
that bees also make conversation . . . through dance?
It's true.

Each boogie-woogie wiggle and buzzing ballet allows them
to talk—bee to bee—about where the best blossoms are.
I like to imagine that every flower they flit to in my
garden is a tiny stage, with a stem.

Making the world a better place through pollination and
performance art—

bravo, bees!

Ants

EKUA HOLMES

When I was a girl, I lived in an apartment where we could not have pets. I wanted a dog or a cat, but the landlord said no. My mother had the idea to get me an ant farm. We put together the bright green plastic set and poured in the sand; the ants arrived later by mail. In their new home, the ants began building, burrowing paths in the sand. I LOVED IT! I could watch them for hours: carrying grains of sand, burrowing pathways, moving food from one location to another, eating and drinking and having babies, which emerged from their tiny cocoons. I wished I was tiny enough to visit them in their homes. I think they were watching me, too.

Ladybug

Tim Hopgood

My favorite bug is a ladybug. I live in England and over here we call ladybugs *ladybirds*, which is a funny name because, as you can see from this drawing, they are not a type of bird. The reason I like ladybugs so much is because of their color—such a bold, bright red—and I love their pretty black spots. And because ladybugs spend most of their time sitting on green leaves, they stand out a mile—which just goes to show, you don't need to be big to be noticed!

Firefly
Kenard Pak

Firefly,
You blink so bright
Float away
Now—
Out of sight!

MARATUS SPECIOSUS

BRENDAN
WENZEL

PEACOCK

MARATUS VOLANS

MARATUS SPLENDENS

SPIDERS

MAKE ME FEEL LIKE ANYTHING IS POSSIBLE.

MILLIPEDES
Britta Teckentrup

I love millipedes! They remind me of my grandmother's garden. I would pick up rocks and stones to find them hiding underneath in the shade.

Did you know that a millipede can have up to 750 legs?

Worker Bee
Eric Fan

My dad became a part-time beekeeper when he retired, and I would watch the bees for hours on end, fascinated by the worker bee's ceaseless industry and organization. It's the worker bee who builds and maintains the hive, feeds the brood, and looks after the queen. As foragers, they leave and return with pollen, nectar, and water for the hive. These worker bees—they are female!

Walking Stick

Eugene Yelchin

I look closely at a tree. Suddenly a twig walks. My heart leaps, first with curiosity, then joy. It's a walking stick, the grand master of disguise. I love them!

RHINO BEETLE

JOEY CHOU

TINY BUG, HUGE STRENGTH.

Rhino beetles can lift something 850 times their own weight.

Eric Carle is the author and illustrator of more than eighty books, including *The Very Hungry Caterpillar* and *Brown Bear, Brown Bear, What Do You See?* written by Bill Martin Jr. Eric was born in the United States but spent his early years in Stuttgart, Germany, where he studied art and design at the Academy of Applied Art. [eric-carle.com]

Denise Fleming is the award-winning author and illustrator of many well-known children's books, including *In the Tall, Tall Grass* and *In the Small, Small Pond*, which received a Caldecott Honor. The illustrations for most of her books were created by pulp painting, a unique paper-making technique. Denise's latest illustrations, including the praying mantis in this book, were created using Denise's recently developed style employing various print-making techniques combined with collage. Denise's love of language is apparent in her writing, which combines rhythm, rhyme, and lots of verbs. She lives in Toledo, Ohio, with her husband, David Powers, with whom she collaborates. [denisefleming.com]

Teagan White is inspired by nature, vintage color, and organic forms. Originally from Chicago, Teagan now lives and works in Minnesota, where she received a BFA in illustration from the Minneapolis College of Art and Design. She spends her tiny amounts of free time following tangled animal paths through forest and field, squishing along reedy riverbanks, attempting to befriend gulls on rocky lakeshores, delighting in the routines of local bunnies and squirrels, picking wildflowers, and collecting animal bones. [teaganwhite.com]

Beth Krommes knew since kindergarten that she would be an artist. She earned degrees in painting and art education and worked at many jobs in the arts. Having children of her own opened her eyes to the world of children's books. Beth received the Caldecott Medal for illustrating *The House in the Night* by Susan Marie Swanson. Her other illustrated books include *Swirl by Swirl: Spirals in Nature* and *Before Morning*, both by Joyce Sidman. She loves to make books that are intriguing for both parents and children. [bethkrommes.com]

Maggie Rudy has been hanging out with animals all her life. She is a multimedia artist and a late-blooming illustrator. She has been making characters and their worlds from felt and scavenged materials for twenty-five years. Maggie lives in Portland, Oregon, where she is known as the Empress of Mouseland. [mouseshouses.blogspot.com]

Scott Magoon likes long-distance running, skiing, gardening, and wandering. He reads a great deal of news, novels, nonfiction, and picture books between fun adventures with his family. They live near Boston, and from there he hones his craft of putting words and pictures together for young readers. He's written and illustrated *Breathe* and *The Boy Who Cried Bigfoot!*, and he's illustrated *Spoon* by Amy Krouse Rosenthal as well as *The Nuts: Bedtime at the Nut House* by Eric Litwin. [scottmagoon.com]

Molly Idle was awarded a Caldecott Honor for *Flora and the Flamingo*. She also is the creator of *Flora and the Penguin* and *Flora and the Peacocks*, as well as the Rex series, which includes *Tea Rex*, *Camp Rex*, and *Sea Rex*. Molly lives in Tempe, Arizona, with her fabulous family. When she's not watching old Technicolor musicals or pottering about in her garden (with the bees), Molly can be found in her workshop with a cup of espresso in one hand and a pencil in the other, working on her next picture book. [idleillustration.com]

Ekua Holmes is a fine artist whose work explores themes of family, relationships, hope, and faith. In 2013 she was named to the Boston Arts Commission, which oversees public art projects on city property. She received a Caldecott Honor for her picture book illustration debut, *Voice of Freedom: Fannie Lou Hamer, Spirit of the Civil Rights Movement*, by Carole Boston Weatherford. Ekua lives in Boston. [ekuaholmes.com]

Tim Hopgood is an award-winning picture-book author and illustrator from England. Having worked as an art director, graphic designer, and copywriter for twenty years, he switched to creating picture books just over ten years ago. His love of color and music has inspired much of his work, which includes the bestselling *WOW! Said the Owl*, *What a Wonderful World*, and *Singing in the Rain*. When he's not in his studio, you'll find him cooking up a storm in the kitchen—or on the dance floor! [timhopgood.com]

Kenard Pak is the author and illustrator of *Goodbye Summer, Hello Autumn* and *Goodbye Autumn, Hello Winter*. A former artist with DreamWorks Animation and Walt Disney Animation Studios, Kenard has also illustrated children's books such as *Have You Heard the Nesting Bird?* by Rita Gray, *The Dinner That Cooked Itself* by J. C. Hsyu, and *The Fog* by Kyo Maclear. He lives in San Francisco with his wife and their cats. [pandagun.com]

Brendan Wenzel is an illustrator based in Brooklyn, New York. His work has appeared internationally in children's books, animations, and magazines. An ardent conservationist, he is a proud collaborator with many organizations working to ensure the future of wild places and threatened species, especially within Southeast Asia. Brendan is a graduate of Pratt Institute. [brendanwenzel.info]

Britta Teckentrup is an award-winning illustrator, author, and fine artist. She was born in Hamburg and grew up in a city called Wuppertal. She moved to London to study illustration and fine art at St. Martin's College and the Royal College of Art. Britta is the author and illustrator of many well-loved books for children, including the bestselling *The Memory Tree* and *Grumpy Cat*. Her books have been published in over twenty different countries. Britta now lives and works in Berlin with her Scottish husband, son Vincent, and their old cat, Oskar. [brittateckentrup.com]

Eric Fan received his formal art training at the Ontario College of Art and Design in Toronto. He collaborates with his brother, Terry, and their debut picture book, *The Night Gardener*, was widely acclaimed. Their work is a blend of traditional and contemporary techniques using ink or graphite mixed with digital tools. Eric has a passion for vintage bikes, clockwork contraptions, and impossible dreams. [thefanbrothers.com]

Eugene Yelchin is the author and illustrator of the middle-grade novels *The Haunting of Falcon House*, *Arcady's Goal*, and the Newbery Honor book *Breaking Stalin's Nose*. He has also illustrated many picture books, including *Spring Hare*; *Crybaby* and *Who Ate All the Cookie Dough?*, both by Karen Beaumont; and *Won Ton* by Lee Wardlaw. He lives in California with his wife and children. [eugeneyelchinbooks.com]

Joey Chou was born in Taiwan and moved to sunny California in his early teens. There he received his BFA from Art Center College of Design in Pasadena. Joey works by day as a visual development artist on animated feature films and by night as a picture-book illustrator. [joeyart.com]